McDougal Littell

Lab Manual

Earth's Surface

McDougal Littell
A HOUGHTON MIFFLIN COMPANY
Evanston, Illinois • Boston • Dallas

Acknowledgment

Adaptation of "A Flow Diagram for Teaching Texture-by-Feel Analysis" by Steve J. Thien, for the *Journal of Agronomic Education,* 1979, vol. 8, pp. 54–55. Copyright © 1979 by Steve J. Thien. Reprinted with permission.

ISBN: 0-618-43726-6

3 4 5 6 7 8 9-MDO-07 06 05

Lab Manual

Table of Contents page

CHAPTER 5 EROSION AND DEPOSITION

CHAPTER 1
Views of Earth Today

SECTION | DATASHEET
1.1 | Investigate Geosphere's Layers

How can you model the geosphere's layers?

MATERIALS: apple slice

PROCEDURE

❶ As a model of the layers in the geosphere, you will be using a quarter of an apple that your teacher has cut. Note: NEVER eat food in the science classroom.

❷ Hold the apple slice and observe it carefully. Compare it with the diagram of the geosphere's layers on page 12.

❸ Draw a diagram of the apple and label it with the names of the layers of the geosphere.

WHAT DO YOU THINK?

What are the four parts of the apple slice?

____

____

What major layer of the geosphere does each part of the apple resemble?

____

____

CHALLENGE

What other object do you think would make a good model of the geosphere's layers? What model could you build or make yourself?

____

____

____

SECTION | DATASHEET

1.2 | Investigate Map Projections

How do you show the curved Earth on a flat surface?

MATERIALS: top 8 inches of 2-liter bottle, marker pen, walnut-sized piece of clay, poster board, flashlight

PROCEDURE

❶ Work in a small group. For a model of the hemisphere, use the top section of a 2-liter plastic bottle that your teacher has cut.

❷ Carefully draw three or four latitude lines and six or eight longitude lines on the bottle.

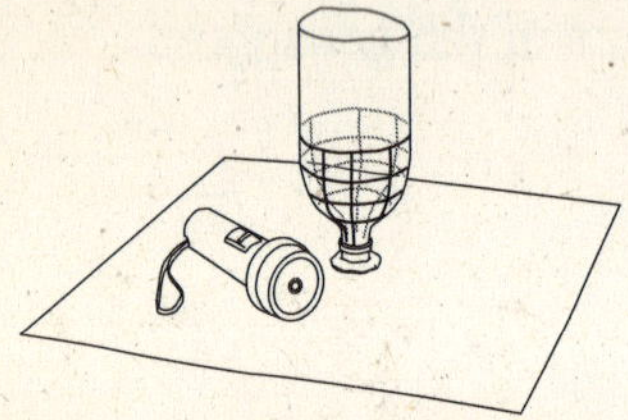

❸ Place a piece of clay in the center of a piece of poster board. Press the bottle top into the clay.

❹ Shine a flashlight above the center of the model. Trace the lines on the poster board to make your projection.

WHAT DO YOU THINK?

What are the similarities and differences between your model and your projection?

____

____

____

____

CHALLENGE

Draw a shape on the plastic bottle to represent a landmass. Use the flashlight again to project the hemisphere. How did the shape of the landmass appear when it was projected onto a flat surface?

____

____

____

SECTION | DATASHEET
1.4 | Investigate Satellite Imaging

How do satellites send images to Earth?

MATERIALS: graph paper, colored pen or pencil

PROCEDURE

1. Work with a partner. One of you will be the "sensor," and the other will be the "receiving station."

2. The sensor draws the initials of a famous person on a piece of graph paper. The receiving station does NOT see the drawing.

3. The sensor sends the picture to the receiving station. For blank squares, the sensor says "Zero." For filled-in squares, the sensor says "One." Be sure to start at the top row and read left to right, telling the receiving station when a row begins.

4. The receiving station transfers the code to the graph paper. At the end, the receiver has three tries to guess whose initials were sent.

WHAT DO YOU THINK?

What would happen if you accidentally skipped or repeated a row?

____

____

If you increased or decreased the number and size of the squares, how would this affect the picture?

____

____

____

CHALLENGE

Use a variety of colors to send other initials or an image. Your code must tell the receiver which code to use for each square.

CHAPTER | CHAPTER INVESTIGATION
1 | Investigate Topographic Maps

OVERVIEW AND PURPOSE

Topographical maps show the shape of the land. In this lab
you will use what you have learned about how Earth's
three-dimensional surface is represented on maps to

- make a terrain model out of clay
- produce a topographic map of the model

Procedure

MATERIALS
- half-gallon cardboard juice container
- scissors
- modeling clay
- clear plastic sheet (transparency or sheet protectors)
- cellophane tape
- ruler
- water
- food coloring
- box of spaghetti
- erasable marker pen

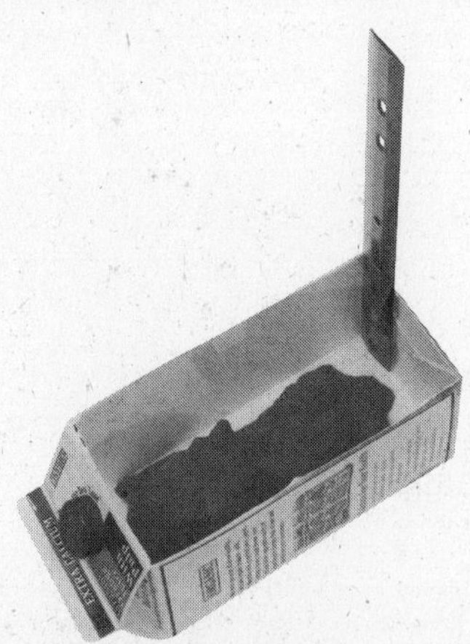

❶ Build a simple landscape about 6–8 cm high from modeling clay. Include a
variety of land features. Make sure your model is no taller than the sides of the
container.

❷ Place your model in the container. Stand a ruler upright inside the container and
tape it in place.

❸ Lay the clear plastic sheet over the container and tape it on one side like a hinge.
Carefully trace the outline of your clay model.

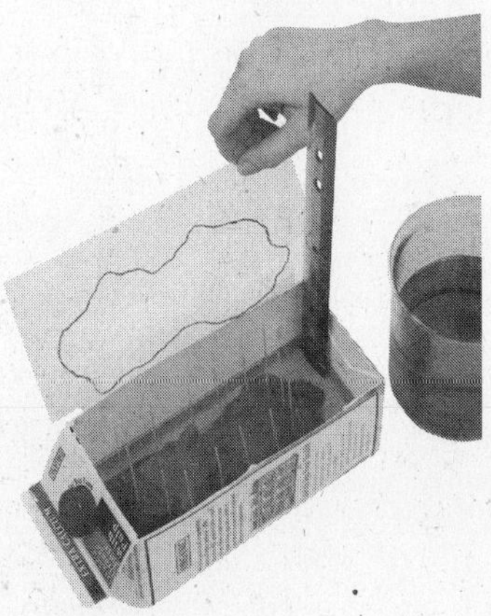

4 Add 2 cm of colored water to the container.

5 Insert spaghetti sticks into the model all around the waterline. Place the sticks about 3 cm apart. Make sure the sticks are straight and are no taller than the sides of the container.

6 Lower the plastic sheet back over the container. Looking straight down on the container, make a dot on the sheet wherever you see a spaghetti stick. Connect the dots to trace the contour line accurately onto your map. See the sample topographic map below as an example of how contour lines may appear.

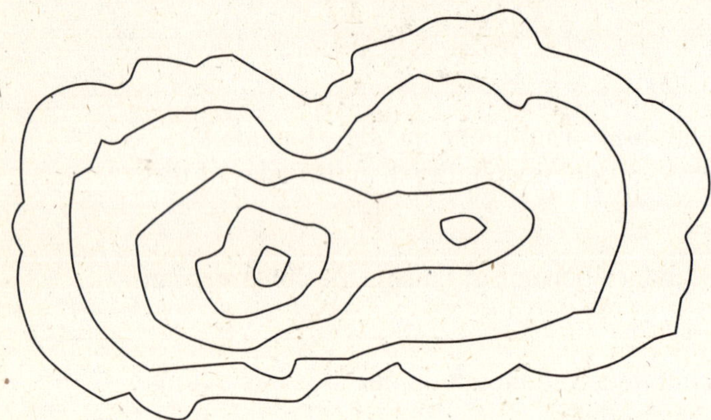

7 Continue adding water, 2 cm at a time. Each time you add water, insert the sticks into the model at the waterline and repeat step 6. Continue until the model landscape is under water. Carefully drain the water when finished.

Observe and Analyze

1. Compare your topographical map with the three-dimensional model. Remember that contour lines connect points of equal elevation. What do widely spaced or tightly spaced contour lines mean? What does a closed circle mean?

2. Make a permanent record of your map to keep in your Science Notebook by carefully tracing the contour lines onto a sheet of white paper. To make reading the map easier, use a different color for the index contour line.

3. What is the contour interval of your model landscape? For example, each 2 centimeters might represent 20 meters on an actual landscape. Record the elevation of your index contour line on your map.

Conclude

1. **Infer** How would you determine the elevation of a point located halfway between two contour lines?

2. **Evaluate** Describe any errors that you may have made in your procedure or any places where errors might have occurred.

3. **Apply** Explain how you would use a topographic map if you were planning a hiking or hiking trip or a cross-country bike race.

CHAPTER 1 | ADDITIONAL INVESTIGATION

Make a Map by Triangulation

OVERVIEW AND PURPOSE

As you know, a map is a scale drawing of Earth on a flat surface. In this lab, you will use what you've learned about maps to

- construct a simple device called a sextant
- use the sextant to make a scale map

Problem

How can you use a straw and a protractor to make a map?

Hypothesize

After step 10 in the procedure, write a hypothesis to explain how you can use your sextant to make a map. Your hypothesis should take the form of an "If . . . , then . . . , because . . . " statement.

Procedure

MATERIALS
- small, thin, metal paper fastener
- pushpin
- hammer
- string, 12 m long
- masking tape
- meter stick
- sharp pencil
- plastic protractor with a small hole in its base
- large plastic straw about 20 cm long
- 2 wooden stakes
- large sheet of plain paper, about 1 m^2

TIME
45 minutes

❶ Use the pushpin to poke a hole through the center of the straw. Carefully push the ends of the metal paper fastner completely through the hole.

❷ Insert the ends of the paper fastener into the hole in the base of the protractor. Secure the straw by spreading the metal ends. Make sure the straw can spin freely. You have made a sighting device called a *sextant*.

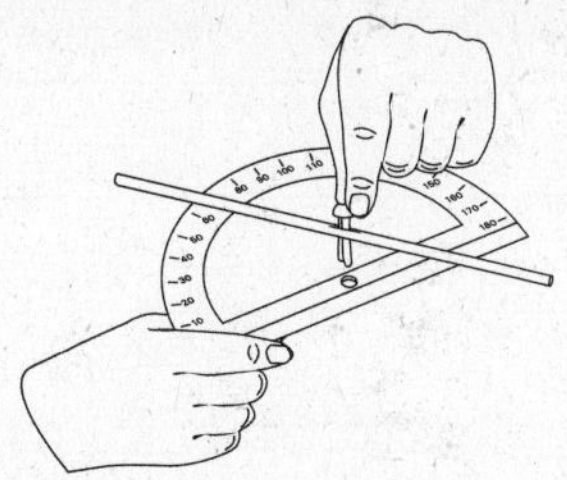

❸ Take your sextant and other materials outdoors. Work with one or two other students to select an area to map. The area that you are going to map should include signposts, trees, a flagpole, playground equipment, or other similar objects.

❹ Use the meter stick to figure out which area you will map. The area should be 10 m × 10 m or smaller.

5 Along one edge of your area, use the string to mark off a baseline. First, use the hammer to push the wooden stakes in the ground. Put one stake at each end of the baseline, as shown in the figure. Make sure that the wooden stakes are the same height above the ground. Pull the string taut and tie each end to a stake.

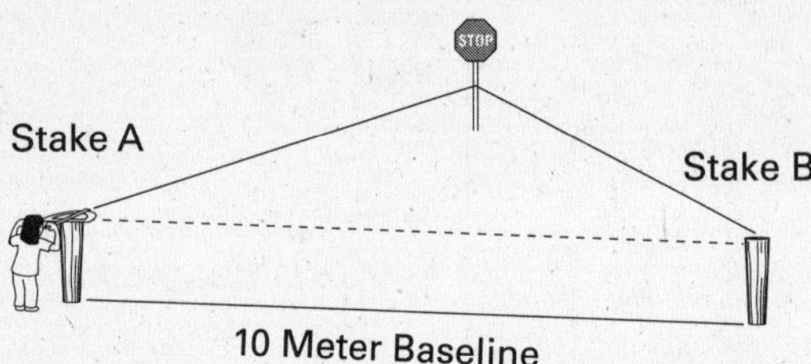

6 Use the meter stick to measure the length of your baseline. Record this measurement in Data Table 1.1.

7 Use the masking tape to secure the sextant to wooden Stake A. The base of the sextant must be parallel to your baseline.

8 Sight an object in your map area through the straw. Record the object and the angle shown on the protractor in the data table.

9 Now secure the sextant to Stake B. Repeat steps 7 and 8, sighting the same object from Stake B. Record the angle shown on the sextant in the third column of the data table.

10 Repeat steps 7 through 9 for many of the large objects in your map area.

DATA TABLE 1.1: ANGLES SHOWN ON SEXTANT		
Object Sighted	**Angle from Stake A**	**Angle from Stake B**

11 Use the meter stick to measure the actual distances between pairs of objects sighted. Record the objects and measurements in Data Table 1,2.

12 Collect all of your materials and take them back inside. Remove the straw from the protractor.

⑬ Use a map scale of 1 cm to 1 m to draw your baseline along the bottom edge of the large sheet of plain paper. Mark the end of each baseline with a small dot. Label these points "Stake A" and "Stake B," as shown in the figure. Make sure your map includes a map scale.

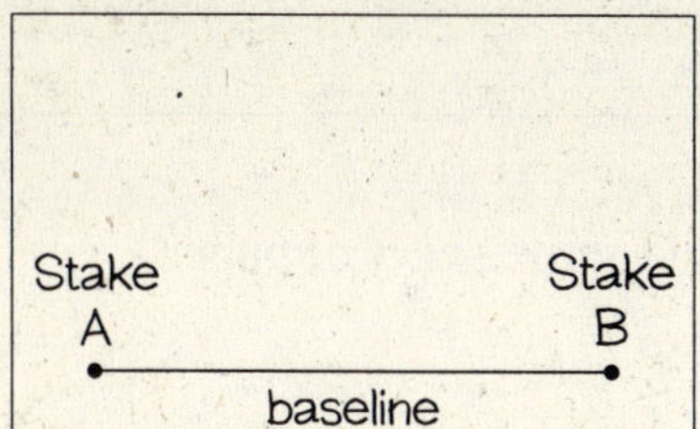

⑭ Place your protractor on the point labeled Stake A. Use a ruler and a pencil to draw the angle for the first object sighted from Stake A. Place your protractor on the point labeled Stake B. Use the ruler to draw the angle for the first object sighted from Stake B. The point where the lines meet is the location of the object. Label this point with the name of the object, such as "flagpole." Erase the lines you drew.

⑮ Repeat step 14 for all of the objects sighted.

⑯ Measure and record in Data Table 1.2 the map distances between pairs of objects.

DATA TABLE 1.2: ACTUAL DISTANCE AND MAP DISTANCE		
Object to Object	**Actual Distance (m)**	**Map Distance (cm)**
Stake to stake (baseline)		

Observe and Analyze

1. Model What is the purpose of your baseline?

____

____

____

2. Compare Compare your map distances for all of the objects sighted with the actual distances. Explain any large differences.

____

____

____

3. Explain Could you have mapped an area twice the size on the same sheet of paper? Explain.

____

____

____

4. Explain The mapping method you used in this investigation is called *triangulation*. Why do you think it is called that name?

____

____

____

Conclude

1. Identify limits How close were the actual distances to your map distances? How might you improve the accuracy of your map?

____

____

____

2. Apply How could you use a sextant to map objects behind a baseline? What would your new sextant look like?

____

____

____

3. Infer If you had mapped a smaller area, would your map have been more accurate or less accurate? Explain why.

____

____

____

SECTION **DATASHEET**
2.1 | Investigate Crystal Shape

How do crystals differ in shape?

MATERIALS: tablespoon, 2 mixing cups, 2 stirring rods, 1 tablespoon table salt,
1 tablespoon Epsom salts, 60 mL water, 2 pie plates, 2 sheets black paper, scissors

PROCEDURE

1. Cut sheets of paper so that they fit inside the pie plates. Place one sheet in each pie plate.

2. Add the table salt to 30 mL of water in the cup. Stir the water until the salt has dissolved.

3. Pour enough salt solution into one of the pie plates to completely cover the paper with a small film of liquid. Be careful not to pour into the plate any undissolved salt that may be in the bottom of the cup.

4. Repeat steps 2 and 3 with the Epsom salts. Let the plates dry overnight.

WHAT DO YOU THINK?

Compare and describe the shapes of the crystals.

____

____

What do you think accounts for any differences you observe?

____

____

CHALLENGE

Why are the shapes of the crystals the same as or different from the shapes in the materials you started with?

____

____

____

____

CHAPTER 2
Minerals

SECTION 2.2 | DATASHEET

Investigate Hardness of Minerals

How hard are some common minerals?

MATERIALS: samples of 5 minerals, copper penny, steel file

PROCEDURE

❶ Try to scratch each mineral with your fingernail, the penny, and the steel file. Record your results below.

❷ Use your results to assign a hardness range in the Mohs scale to each sample.

Mohs Scale

1	2	3	4	5	6	7	8	9	10
Talc	Gypsum	Calcite	Fluorite	Apatite	Feldspar	Quartz	Topaz	Corundum	Diamond

❸ In the last column of the chart, rank the minerals from hardest to softest.

	Mineral	Fingernail	Penny	Steel File	Hardness Range	Rank
1						
2						
3						
4						
5						

WHAT DO YOU THINK?

If two minerals have the same hardness range according to your tests, how could you tell which is harder?

CHALLENGE

If you had a mineral that could not be scratched by the steel file, what might you test it with to estimate its hardness?

SECTION | DATASHEET
2.3 | Investigate Mining

What are the benefits and costs of mining ores?

MATERIALS: 1 pound wild-birdseed mix with sunflower seeds, shallow pan, 2 small red beads, 4 small green beads, 8 small blue beads, 3 medium yellow beads

PROCEDURE

❶ Put the wild-birdseed into a pan. Add the beads to the birdseed and mix well.

❷ Search through the seeds and separate the beads and sunflower seeds, placing each kind in a different pile. Take no more than 3 minutes.

❸ Assign a value to each of the beads and seeds: red bead, $5; green bead, $4; blue bead, $3; and sunflower seeds, $2. Count the value of your beads and seeds. For every yellow bead, subtract $100, which represents the cost of restoring the land after mining.

WHAT DO YOU THINK?

How does the difficulty of finding the red beads relate to the difficulty of finding the most valuable ores?

____

How does the total value of the blue beads and the sunflower seeds compare to the total value of the red and green beads? What can you conclude about deciding which materials to mine?

____

____

CHALLENGE

The sunflower seeds and the red, green, and blue beads could represent minerals that contain copper, gold, iron, and silver. Which bead or seed is most likely to represent which mineral? Explain your choices.

____

____

CHAPTER | DATASHEET

2 | Mineral Identification Key

In this table, minerals are arranged in order of increasing hardness. The most useful properties for identification are printed in *italic* type. The colors listed are the most common for each mineral.

Name	Hardness	Color	Streak	Cleavage	Remarks
Talc	*1*	Apple-green, gray, white	White	Perfect in one direction	Nonmetallic (pearly to greasy) luster. Nonelastic flakes, *greasy feel.* Sp. gr. 2.7 to 2.8.
Graphite	1–2	*Dark gray to black*	Grayish black	*Perfect in one direction*	Metallic or nonmetallic (earthy) luster. *Greasy feel, marks paper.* This is the "lead" in a pencil (mixed with clay). Sp. gr. 2.2.
Gypsum	*2*	Colorless, white, gray, yellowish, reddish	White	*Perfect in one direction*	Nonmetallic (glassy to silky) luster. *Can be scratched easily by a fingernail.* Sp. gr. 2.3.
Halite	2–2.5	Colorless, white	White	*Perfect, three directions, at 90° angles*	Nonmetallic (glassy) luster. *Salty taste.* Sp. gr. 2.2.
Muscovite mica	2–2.5	Colorless in thin films; silvery, yellowish, and greenish in thicker pieces	*White*	Perfect in one direction	Nonmetallic (glassy to pearly) luster. *Thin elastic films peel off readily.* Sp. gr. 2.8 to 2.9.
Galena	2.5	*Lead gray*	Lead gray	*Perfect, three directions, at 90° angles*	*Metallic luster.* Occurs as crystals and masses. *Dense.* Sp. gr. 7.4 to 7.6.
Biotite mica	2.5–3	Black, brown, dark green	White	*Perfect in one direction*	Nonmetallic (glassy) luster. *Thin elastic films peel off easily.* Sp. gr. 2.8 to 3.2.
Copper	2.5–3	*Copper red*	Copper	None	*Metallic luster on fresh surface. Dense.* Sp. gr. 8.9.
Calcite	*3*	White, colorless	White	*Perfect, three directions, not at 90° angles*	Nonmetallic (glassy to dull) luster. *Fizzes in dilute hydrochloric acid.* Sp. gr. 2.7.
Chalcopyrite	3.5–4	*Golden yellow*	Greenish black	Poor in one direction	Metallic luster. *Hardness distinguishes from pyrite.* Sp. gr. 4.1 to 4.3.
Dolomite	3.5–4	Pinkish, colorless, white	White	*Perfect, three directions, not at 90° angles*	Nonmetallic luster. *Scratched surface fizzes in dilute hydrochloric acid. Cleavage surfaces curved.* Sp. gr. 2.8 to 2.9.

Name	Hardness	Color	Streak	Cleavage	Remarks
Sphalerite	*3.5–4*	*Yellow, brown, black*	Yellow to light brown	*Perfect, six directions*	*Nonmetallic (brilliant to resinous) luster.* Sp. gr. 3.9 to 4.1.
Fluorite	4	Varies	White	*Perfect, four directions*	Nonmetallic (glassy) luster. In cubes or octahedrons as crystals. Sp. gr. 3.2.
Apatite	5	Green, brown	White	Poor in one direction	Nonmetallic (glassy) luster. Sp. gr. 3.1 to 3.2.
Augite	5–6	Dark green to black	Greenish	*Two directions nearly at 90°*	Nonmetallic (glassy) luster. *Stubby four- or eight-sided crystals.* Common type of pyroxene. Sp. gr. 3.2 to 3.4.
Hematite	5–6 (may appear softer)	*Reddish-brown, gray, black*	*Reddish*	None	Metallic or nonmetallic (earthy) luster. *Dense.* Sp. gr. 5.3.
Hornblende	5–6	*Dark green to black*	Brown to gray	*Perfect, two directions at angles of 56° and 124°*	Nonmetallic (glassy to silky) luster. Common type of amphibole. Long, slender, six-sided crystals. Sp. gr. 3.0 to 3.4.
Magnetite	5.5–6.5	*Black*	Black	None	Metallic luster. Occurs as eight-sided crystals and granular masses. *Magnetic. Dense.* Sp. gr. 5.2.
Feldspar (Orthoclase)	6	*Salmon pink, red, white, light gray*	White	*Good, two directions, 90° intersection*	Nonmetallic (glassy) luster. *Hardness, color, and cleavage taken together are diagnostic.* Sp. gr. 2.6.
Feldspar (Plagioclase)	6	*White to light gray,* can be salmon pink	White	*Good, two directions, about 90°*	Nonmetallic (glassy or pearly) luster. *If striations are visible, they are diagnostic.* Sp. gr. 2.6 to 2.8.
Pyrite	*6–6.5*	*Brass yellow*	Greenish black	None	Metallic luster. *Cubic crystals* and granular masses. *Dense.* Sp. gr. 5.0 to 5.1.
Olivine	6.5–7	*Yellowish, greenish*	White	None	*Nonmetallic (glassy) luster. Granular.* Sp. gr. 3.3 to 4.4.
Quartz	*7*	*Colorless, white; varies*	White	None	Nonmetallic (glassy) luster. *Conchoidal fracture. Six-sided crystals common.* Many varieties. Sp. gr. 2.6.
Topaz	*8*	Varies	White	Perfect in one direction	Nonmetallic (brilliant to glassy) luster. *Crystals commonly striated length-wise.* Sp. gr. 3.4 to 3.6.
Corundum	9	Brown, pink, blue	White	None, parting resembles cleavage	Nonmetallic (glassy to brilliant) luster. *Barrel-shaped, six-sided crystals with flat ends.* Sp. gr. 4.0.

Sp. gr. = specific gravity

CHAPTER | DATASHEET
2 | # Mohs Scale

Mohs Scale
1 Talc
2 Gypsum
3 Calcite
4 Fluorite
5 Apatite
6 Feldspar
7 Quartz
8 Topaz
9 Corundum
10 Diamond

CHAPTER INVESTIGATION

Mineral Identification

OVERVIEW AND PURPOSE

In this activity, you will observe and perform tests on minerals. Then you will compare your observations to a mineral identification key.

Procedure

1. You will examine and identify five minerals. Get a numbered mineral sample from the mineral set. Record the number of your sample in your data table below.

MATERIALS
- numbered mineral samples
- hand lens
- streak plate
- copper penny
- steel file
- magnet
- dilute hydrochloric acid
- eyedropper
- Moh's scale
- Mineral Identification Key

CHAPTER 2
Minerals

TABLE 1. MINERAL PROPERTIES

Property	Sample Number				
	1	2	3	4	5
Color					
Luster					
Cleavage					
Fracture					
Streak					
Hardness					
Special Tests					
Magnetic					
Acid Test					
Name of Mineral					

❷ First, observe the sample. Note the color and the luster of the sample. Write these observations in your data table. In the row marked "Luster," write metallic if the mineral appears shiny like metal. Write non-metallic if the sample does not look like metal. For example, it may look glassy, pearly, or dull.

❸ Observe the sample through the hand lends. Look to see any signs of how the crystals in the mineral broke. If it appears that the crystal has broken along straight lines, put a check in the row marked "Cleavage." If it appears that the sample has fractured, put a check in that row on your data table.

❹ CAUTION: Keep the streak plate on your desktop or table while you are doing the streak test. A broken streak plate can cause serious cuts. Rub the mineral sample across the streak plate. If the sample doesn't leave a mark, the sample is harder than the streak plate. Write *No* in the row labeled "Streak." If the sample does leave a mark on the streak plate, write the color of the streak in that row.

❺ Test each of the samples for hardness according to Moh's hardness scale. Try to scratch the sample with each of these items in order: your fingernail, a copper penny, and a steel file. Using Moh's scale, find the hardness number for the object that first scratches the sample. Write in the data table that the mineral's hardness value is between that of the hardest item that did not scratch the sample and that of the item that did scratch it.

TABLE 2. MOH'S HARDNESS SCALE		
Talc	1	Scratched by a fingernail
Gypsum	2	
Calcite	3	Scratched by a copper coin
Fluorite	4	Scratched by a knife blade or window glass
Apatite	5	
Feldspar	6	Scratches a knife blade or window glass
Quartz	7	
Topaz	8	
Corundum	9	
Diamond	10	Scratches all common materials

6 Test each of the samples with the magnet. If the sample is attracted to the magnet, put a checkmark in the row marked "Magnetic."

7 Repeat steps 1 through 6 for each of the numbered samples.

Observe and Analyze

1. **Interpret Data** Use the Mineral Identification Key and the information in your data table to identify your samples. Write the names of the minerals on your data table.

2. **Collect Data** CAUTION: Before doing the acid test, put on your safety glasses, protective gloves, and lab apron. Acids can cause burns. If you identified one of the samples as a carbonate mineral, such as calcite, you can check your identification with the acid test. Use the eyedropper to put a few drops of dilute hydrochloric acid on the mineral. If the acid bubbles, the sample is a carbonate.

Conclude

1. **Compare and Contrast** How are the minerals calcite and halite alike? Which property can you use to test whether a sample is calcite or halite?

   ____

   ____

   ____

   ____

2. **Interpret** Look at the results on your data table. Name any minerals that you could identify on the basis of a single property.

   ____

   ____

   ____

   ____

3. **Apply** Examine a piece of granite rock. On the basis of your examination of granite and your observations of the samples, try to determine what the light-colored, translucent mineral in the granite is and what the flaky, darker mineral is.

   ____

   ____

   ____

   ____

11 Below, draw a side view of your "cave" two or three days after you made it. Draw the same view after 5 days. Draw the "cave" again after a week or so.

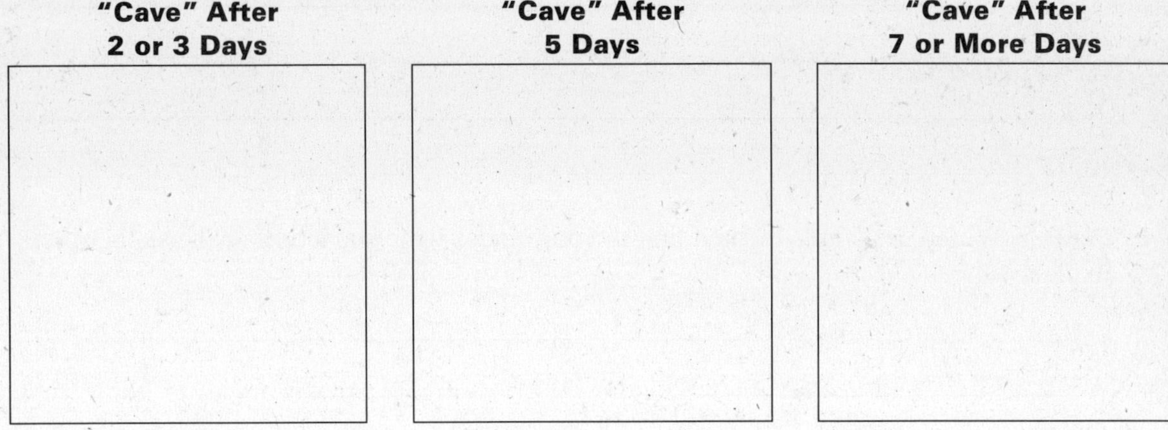

Observe and Analyze

1. **Explain** Why was it helpful to add such large amounts of Epsom salts to the hot tap water?

2. **Explain** Why was it important that the yarn not touch the outsides of the cups?

3. **Observe** Stalactites are structures that hang from the ceilings of a cave. Explain how your stalactites formed.

4. **Observe** Stalagmites are structures that "grow" upward from a cave's floor. Explain how your stalagmites formed.

____

____

____

5. **Explain** Which structures formed first in your model—the stalactites or the stalagmites? Explain why.

____

____

____

6. **Compare** Observe the shapes of your stalactites and stalagmites. How are they the same? How do they differ?

____

____

____

Conclude

1. **Predict** Predict how you could increase the rate of mineral formation in this investigation.

____

____

____

2. **Apply** How could you increase the size of the mineral crystals that form in the cave?

____

____

____

3. **Draw Conclusions** In this investigation, you added the minerals (Epsom salts) to the water to form the solution. Where do the dissolved minerals that form structures in an actual cave come from?

____

____

____

____

SECTION | DATASHEET

3.1 | Investigate Classification of Rocks

How can rocks be classified?

MATERIALS 5 rock samples

PROCEDURE

❶ Examine the rock samples. Look at their physical characteristics.

❷ Make a list on a separate sheet of paper of the differences in the physical characteristics of the rocks.

❸ Use your list to decide which characteristics of the rocks are most important in classifying the rocks into different types. Write the five most important characteristics in the spaces below the *Characteristics* heading. Complete the chart showing the different rock characteristics. Then classify the rocks into types by using the chart.

CHARACTERISTICS					
Rock					
1					
2					
3					
4					
5					

WHAT DO YOU THINK?

Which physical characteristic is most helpful in classifying the rocks?

____

Which physical characteristic is least helpful in classifying the rocks?

____

CHALLENGE

Is it possible to classify rocks only by the characteristics you can see?

____

____

3.2 | Mineral Crystal Diagrams

Match each rock diagram with the graph that shows how quickly it cooled.

Igneous
Rock A

Description ________________

____

____

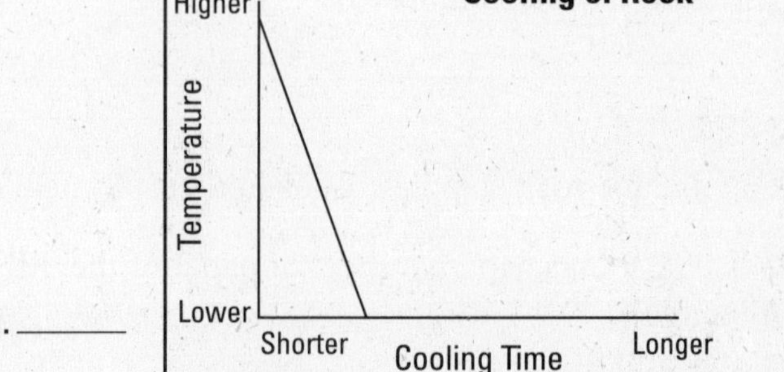

1. ________

Description ________________

____

____

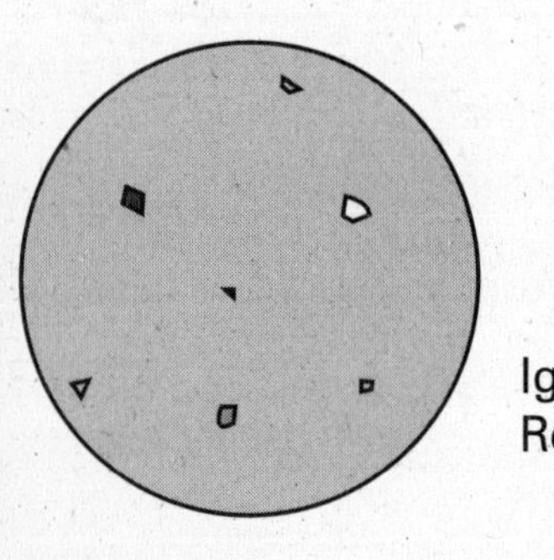

Igneous
Rock B

Description ________________

____

____

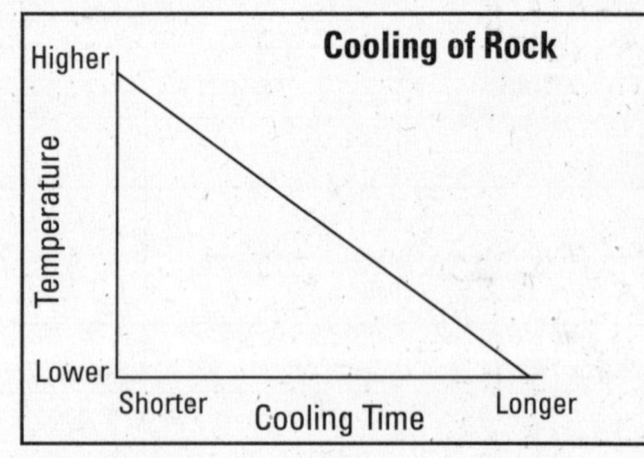

2. ________

Description ________________

____

____

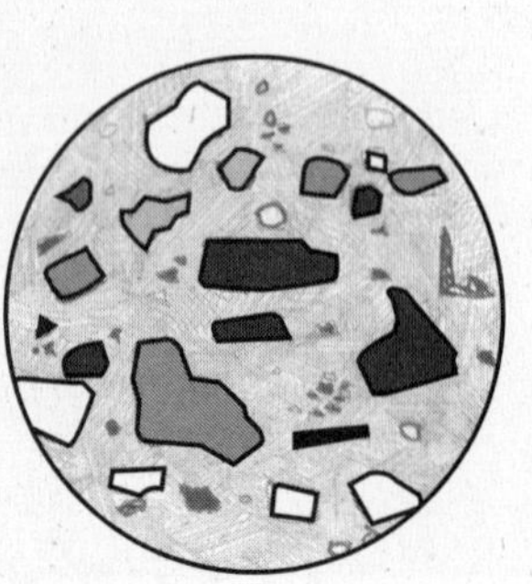

Igneous
Rock C

Description ________________

____

____

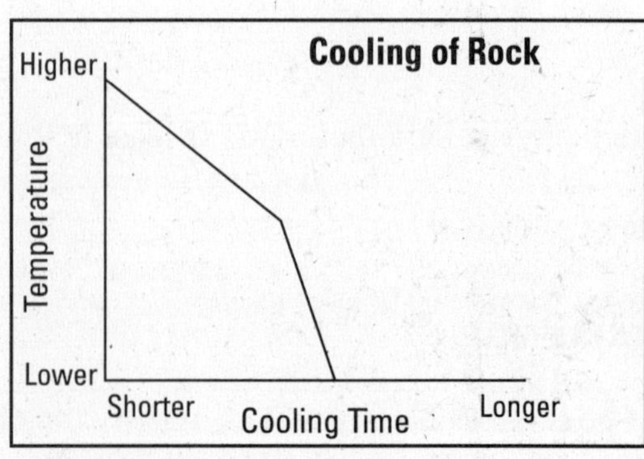

3. ________

Description ________________

____

____

SECTION | DATASHEET
3.2 | Investigate Crystal Size

How does cooling time affect crystal size?

MATERIALS Mineral Crystal Diagrams datasheet

PROCEDURE

1. Look at the Mineral Crystal Diagrams datasheet.

2. Describe your observations of the crystals in each of the igneous-rock diagrams A–C on the lines provided.

3. Describe what is shown in each of graphs 1–3 on the lines provided.

4. Match each igneous-rock diagram with its corresponding diagram.

5. On the back of the paper, explain why you matched each crystal diagram with a particular graph.

WHAT DO YOU THINK?

Which diagram shows an intrusive igneous rock, such as gabbro?

____

____

Where do you think the rock shown in diagram B formed? Explain your answer.

____

____

____

CHALLENGE

Write a hypothesis to explain why the rock shown in diagram C might be found at a shallow depth in Earth's crust.

____

____

____

SECTION **3.3** | DATASHEET

Investigate Rock Layers

How do sedimentary rocks form in layers?

MATERIALS 1 paper cup, 3 mixing cups, 6 tbs plaster of Paris, 3 tbs water, 4 tbs gravel, 2 tbs sand, 3 drops of food coloring

PROCEDURE

1. Prepare the plaster of Paris by mixing it with the water.

2. Mix 2 tablespoons of the gravel or pebbles with 2 tablespoons of the plaster of Paris and pour the mixture into the paper cup.

3. Mix the sand with 2 tablespoons of the plaster of Paris and the food coloring. Add the mixture to the paper cup on top of the gravel mixture.

4. Mix the rest of the gravel with the rest of the plaster of Paris. Add the mixture to the paper cup, on top of the sand mixture.

5. After the mixture hardens for about 5 minutes, tear apart the paper cup and observe the layers.

WHAT DO YOU THINK?

How is the procedure you used to make your model similar to the way sedimentary rock forms?

____

____

Describe how similar layers of real rock could form.

____

____

____

____

CHALLENGE

How would you create a model to show the formation of fossil-rich limestone?

____

____

SECTION | DATASHEET
3.4 | Investigate Metamorphic Changes

How can pressure and temperature change a solid?

MATERIALS 3 candles of different colors, vegetable peeler

PROCEDURE

❶ Use a vegetable peeler to make a handful of wax shavings of three colors. Mix the shavings.

❷ Use your hands to warm the shavings, and then squeeze them into a wafer.

WHAT DO YOU THINK?

Describe what happened to the wax shavings.

____

____

How do the changes you observed resemble metamorphic changes in rocks?

____

____

____

____

CHALLENGE

What changes that occur in metamorphic rocks were you unable to model in this experiment?

____

____

3 | Rock Classification Key

Match each rock diagram with the graph that shows how quickly it cooled.

1. **Look at the composition of your rock. Is the rock made up of visible particles (for example, mineral crystals or sand)?**

   a. Some or all of the particles are visible. [go to step 3]

   b. The rock does not contain any visible particles. [go to step 2]

2. **Look at the texture of your rock. Is the rock glassy, porous (sponge-like), or completely solid?**

   a. The rock is glassy or porous. [the rock is igneous]

   b. The rock is completely solid. [go to step 5]

3. **Determine the type of particles that make up the rock.**

   a. The rock has visible mineral crystals. [go to step 4]

   b. The rock is made up of individual particles (such as sand or pebbles) that are cemented together. [the rock is sedimentary]

4. **Determine if the mineral crystals of the rock tend to line up or form bands.**

   a. The mineral crystals are not lined up in any particular direction. [go to step 7]

   b. The mineral crystals tend to line up or to form bands. [the rock is metamorphic]

5. **Determine if the rock is made up of layers or if it tends to break into layers.**

   a. The rock has no layers and does not break into layers. [the rock is igneous]

   b. The rock has layers or tends to break into layers. [go to step 6]

6. **Determine how shiny the rock is.**

   a. The rock is not shiny. [the rock is sedimentary]

   b. The rock is somewhat to quite shiny. [the rock is metamorphic]

7. **Determine if the rock is made up of one or more types of mineral crystals.**

   a. All the crystals appear to be of the same mineral. [the rock is metamorphic]

   b. The crystals are of two or more types of minerals. [the rock is igneous]

 | CHAPTER INVESTIGATION
Rock Classification

OVERVIEW AND PURPOSE

In this activity, you will examine rock samples and refer to a rock classification key. You will classify each sample as igneous, sedimentary, or metamorphic.

MATERIALS
- magnifying lens
- 6–8 rock samples
- Rock Classification Key

Procedure

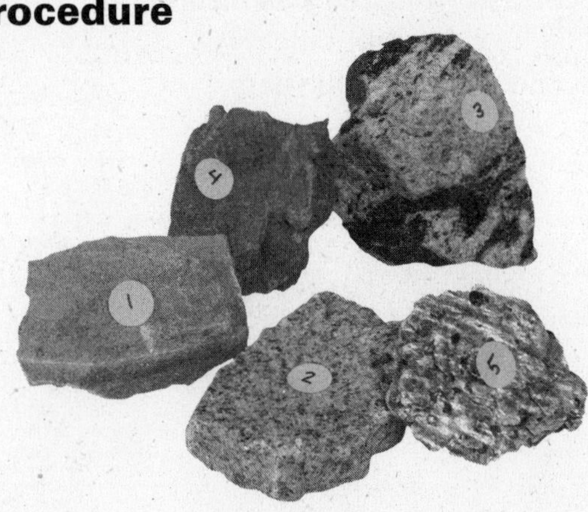

❶ Get a numbered rock sample. Record its number in the table below.

TABLE 1		
Sample Number	**Description of Its Visible Properties**	**Rock Class**

2 Observe the sample as a whole. Then closely examine it with the hand lens. Record in your table all visual properties of the sample. For example, include properties such as mineral or sediment size, layering, or banding.

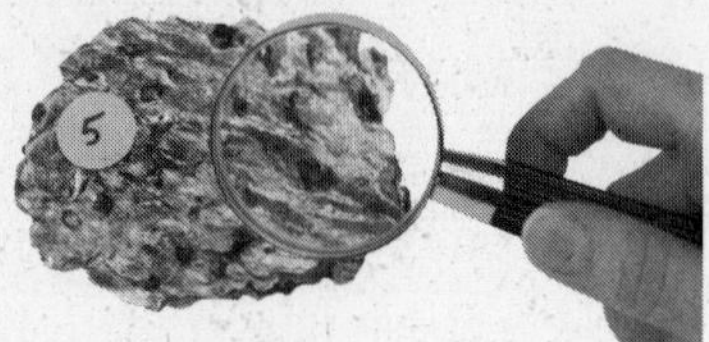

3 Look at the classification key. Each item in the key consists of paired statements. Start with item 1 of the key. Choose the statement that best describes the rock you are examining. Look at the end of the statement and then go to the item number indicated.

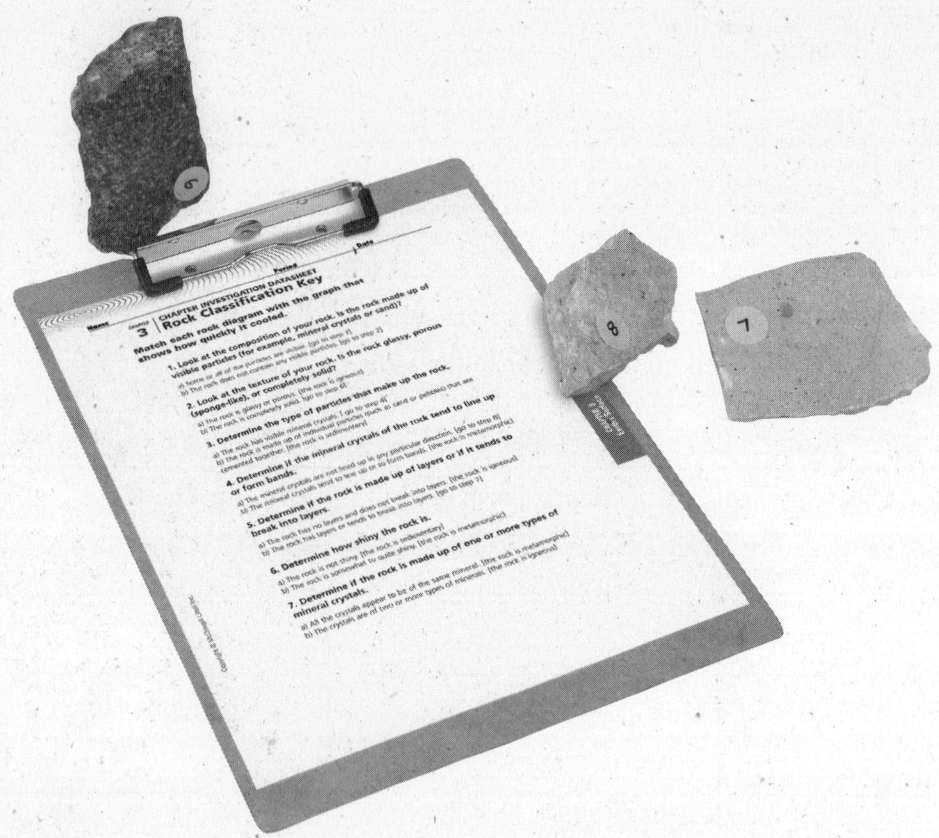

4 Examine the rock sample again and choose the statement that best describes the rock.

5 Continue to work through the key until your choices lead you to a classification that fits your rock. Repeat steps 1–4 for each of the numbered samples.

Observe and Analyze

1. **Interpret** Referring to the Rock Classification Key and the observations you recorded, write the type of each rock in your data table.

2. **Identify Limits** What problems, if any, did you experience in applying the key? Which samples did not seem to fit easily into a category? How could you improve the key?

____

____

____

____

Conclude

1. **Compare and Contrast** How are igneous and metamorphic rocks similar? How can you tell them apart?

____

____

____

2. **Analyze** Examine a sample of sedimentary rock in which visible particles are cemented together. In addition to sight, what other sense could help you classify the rock sample? Explain your answer.

____

____

3. **Apply** What have you learned from this investigation that would help you make a classification key that someone else could follow? How would you make a key to classify a music collection? Write two pairs of numbered statements that would start the classification process.

____

____

____

____

CHAPTER 3
Rocks

CHAPTER 3 | ADDITIONAL INVESTIGATION

Modeling Rock Formation

OVERVIEW AND PURPOSE

As you know, different rocks form in different ways. In this investigation, you will use what you've learned about rocks to

- model some of the ways in which rocks form
- identify the rocks represented by your models

Problem

How can you model some of the processes that form rocks?

Hypothesize

Read the materials list. Write a hypothesis to explain how you can use the materials to model different ways in which rocks form. What kinds of rocks can you model?

____

____

____

____

____

____

MATERIALS

- 20 small thin candles
- plastic knife
- 3 small aluminum pans
- hot plate
- tongs
- 10 small plastic craft beads—all different shapes
- 400-mL beaker half full of cold tap water
- modeling clay (about 250 g)
- 20 small plastic craft beads—long
- waxed paper
- rolling pin
- salt (about 100 g)
- 2 craft sticks
- sand grains (about 75 g)
- pea gravel (about 25 g)
- spoon
- white glue
- 2 small paper cups

TIME: 45 minutes

Procedure

❶ Put on your safety goggles and lab apron. Leave them on until you have *completely* finished this investigation.

❷ Cut the candles into small pieces. Remove the wicks. Put half of the pieces into one of the small pans. Put the rest of the pieces into the other pan. Put the pans on the hot plate.

❸ Once you have your teacher's permission to use the hot plate, turn it on high. **CAUTION:** Be careful when using any heat source.

❹ When the wax has completely melted, turn off the hot plate. Use the tongs to remove one of the pans. Put the pan aside. Put the irregularly shaped craft beads into this pan.

⑤ Use the tongs to remove the other pan from the hot plate. Turn the hot plate off. Carefully and slowly pour the melted wax into the beaker of cold water. Don't let the melted wax touch the sides of the beaker.

⑥ After about 10 minutes, observe the wax in both containers. Record your observations in the data table.

⑦ Warm the modeling clay with your hands. Roll the clay into a large ball. Place the small, long craft beads into the ball. Make sure the craft beads are spread throughout the clay.

⑧ Put the ball of clay between two pieces of waxed paper. Use the rolling pin to flatten the clay into a rectangle.

⑨ Remove the clay from the waxed paper. Study the clay. Record your observations in the data table.

⑩ Put the salt into one of the pans. Add just enough water to dissolve the salt while stirring with a craft stick. Put the pan back on the hot plate.

⑪ Repeat step 3.

⑫ Heat until all the water has evaporated. Use the tongs to remove the pan, and put it aside. Turn the hot plate off.

⑬ Put the sand grains, the pea gravel, and two spoons of white glue into the other small paper cup. Mix the materials with a craft stick.

⑭ After the glue has completely dried, tear the cup off of the hardened mixture. Observe the mixture and record your observations in the data table.

DATA TABLE 3.1: MODELING ROCK-FORMING PROCESSES	
Process	**Observations**
melting candle wax	
flattening a ball of clay	
Recrystallizing salt	
mixing sand, gravel, and glue	

Observe and Analyze

1. **Model** What type of "rock" did you make in steps 2–5?

   ____

2. **Explain** What rock cycle processes did you model in steps 2–5?

   ____

   ____

   ____

3. **Model** What type of "rock" did you make in steps 7–9?

   ____

4. **Explain** What rock cycle processes did you model in steps 7–9?

   ____

   ____

   ____

5. **Model** What type of "rocks" did you make in steps 10–13?

   ____

6. **Explain** What rock cycle processes did you model in steps 10–13?

   ____

   ____

   ____

**CHAPTER 3
Rocks**

Conclude

1. **Apply** What similarities exist between the processes that form igneous and metamorphic rocks? What is the major difference in how these two types of rocks form?

   ____

   ____

   ____

2. **Apply** How do the processes that form sedimentary rocks differ from those that result in igneous and metamorphic rocks?

   ____

   ____

   ____

3. **Identify Limits** How was this investigation similar to the formation of actual rocks? How was it different?

   ____

   ____

   ____

4. **Synthesize** Use what you know about rocks to describe how a sedimentary rock can form from a deeply buried igneous rock.

   ____

   ____

   ____

4.1 Investigate Chemical Weathering

What is necessary for rust to form?

MATERIALS: steel wool, 3 cups, water

PROCEDURE

1. Place a piece of steel wool in a cup filled to the top with water. Place a second piece of steel wool in a cup with a small amount of water. The water should touch but not cover the steel wool. Place a third piece in a cup with no water.

2. Allow the three cups to sit overnight. Observe the appearance of the steel wool in each container the next day.

WHAT DO YOU THINK?

1. What happened to the steel wool in each cup?

____

____

____

2. Judging by the appearance of the pieces of steel wool, what do you think is necessary for rusting to occur?

____

____

CHALLENGE

Tear the steel wool that rusted most apart and compare the appearances of the inside and the outside. Why might the inside and the outside look different?

____

____

____

SECTION | DATASHEET
4.3 | Apple Chart

Use the chart below as you complete the activity. The first column contains a description of each step. The second column describes what each step represents. In the third column, draw a picture of what your apple looks like at each step.

Description of step	What does it represent?	Drawing
1. Cut the apple into quarters and set aside three of the quarters.	• The three quarters you set aside represent the amount of Earth that is covered by the ocean. • The one quarter left over represents all the land on Earth that is above the ocean.	
2. Cut the one quarter that represents Earth's land in half. Set aside one of these pieces.	• The piece you set aside represents land too hot, cold, steep, wet, dry or otherwise uninhabitable by people. • The other piece represents the land where people live.	
3. Cut the piece that represents the land where people live into four sections. Set aside three sections.	• The three pieces you set aside represent land that cannot support food crops.	
4. Peel the skin off of the remaining one section.	• The peel represents the amount of land on Earth with fertile soil, capable of supporting agriculture. • It is this tiny portion of land that humans rely on for almost all food production.	

SECTION | DATASHEET
4.3 | Investigate Soil Conservation

How can you model Earth's soil with an apple?

MATERIALS: Apple Chart, apple, plastic knife

PROCEDURE

❶ Fill in a row of the Apple Chart as you complete each step.

❷ Cut the apple into quarters. Set aside three of the quarters.

❸ Cut the remaining quarter in half. Set aside one of these pieces.

❹ Cut the remaining piece from step 3 into four pieces. Set aside three of them.

❺ Peel the skin off the remaining piece from step 4.

WHAT DO YOU THINK?

1. How does the amount of fertile soil on Earth compare with what you expected?

____

____

2. Do you think that the amount of fertile soil on Earth is increasing or decreasing? Explain your answer.

____

____

____

CHALLENGE

Invent a method of soil conservation other than the ones you have read about. How would your method help keep soil in place?

____

____

____

Texture Flow Chart

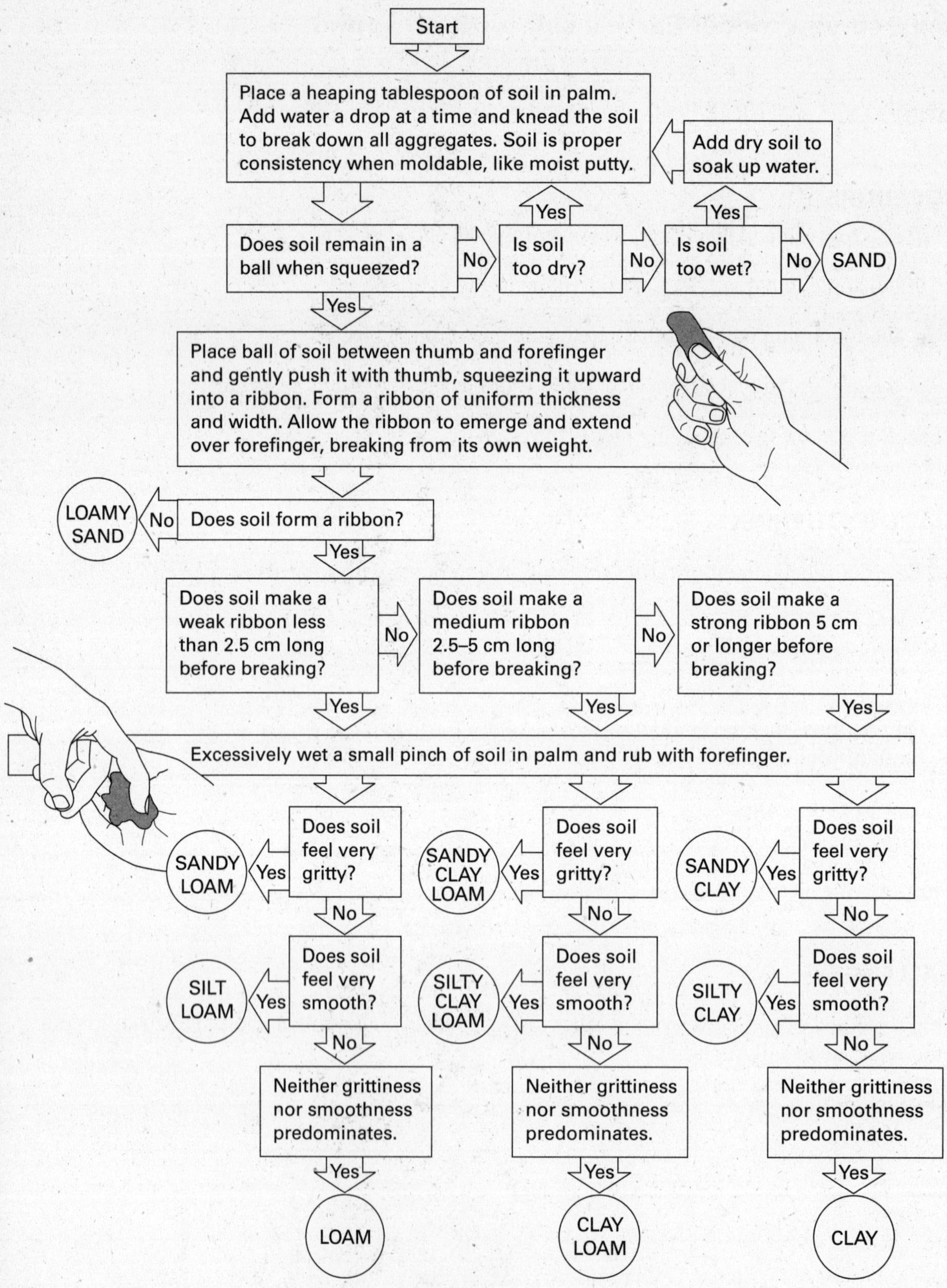

 CHAPTER INVESTIGATION

Testing Soil

OVERVIEW AND PURPOSE

Soil is necessary for life. Whether a soil is suitable for farming or construction, and whether it absorbs water when it rains, depends on the particular properties of that soil. In this investigation you will

- test a soil sample to measure several soil properties
- identify the properties of your soil sample

Procedure

PORE-SPACE TEST

MATERIALS
- dried soil sample
- 250-mL graduated cylinder
- 1-qt jar with lid
- water
- 2-L plastic bottle
- scissors
- window screening
- rubber band
- pH test strips
- clock with second hand

❶ Measure 200 mL of the dried soil sample in a graduated cylinder. Pour it into the jar.

❷ Rinse the graduated cylinder, then fill it with 200 mL of water. Slowly pour the water into the jar until the soil is so soaked that any additional water would pool on top.

❸ Record the amount of water remaining in the graduated cylinder. Then determine by subtraction the amount you added to the soil sample. Record this number in Table 1.

TABLE 1. SOIL PROPERTIES CHART		
Property	**Result**	**Notes and Calculations**
Pore space	_____mL water added	
pH	before: pH = _____ after: pH = _____	
Drainage	_____ seconds	
Particle type	height of sand = _____cm height of silt = _____cm height of clay = _____cm total height = _____cm	

❹ Discard the wet soil according to your teacher's instructions, and rinse the jar.

pH TEST AND DRAINAGE TEST

❺ Cut off the top of a plastic bottle and use a rubber band to attach a piece of window screening over its mouth. Place the bottle top, mouth down, into the jar.

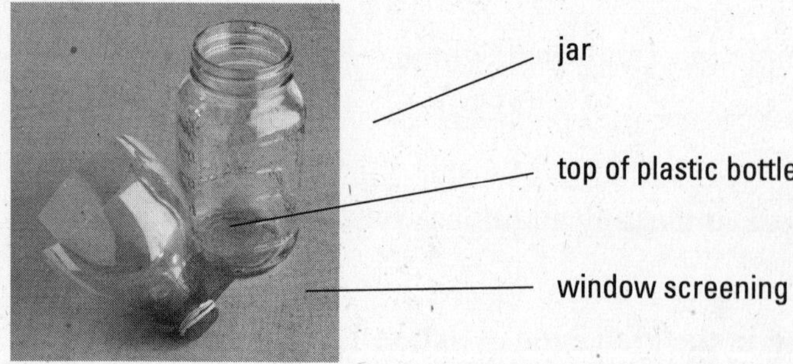

❻ Use the graduated cylinder to measure 200 mL of soil. Pour the soil into the inverted bottle top.

7 Rinse the graduated cylinder, and fill it with 100 mL of water. Test the water's pH, using a pH test strip. Record the result in the "before" space in your soil properties chart.

8 Pour the water into the soil. Measure the amount of time it takes for the first drips to fall into the jar. Record the result in Table 1.

9 Once the water stops dripping, remove the bottle top. Use a new pH strip to measure the pH of the water in the jar. Record this measurement in the "after" space in Table 1 and note any differences in the appearance of the water before and after its filtering through the soil.

10 Discard the wet soil according to your teacher's instructions, and rinse the jar.

PARTICLE-TYPE TEST

11 Add water to the jar until it is two-thirds full. Pour in soil until the water level rises to the top of the jar, then replace the lid. Shake the jar, and set it to rest undisturbed on a countertop overnight.

12 The next day, observe the different soil layers. The sample should have separated into sand (on the bottom), silt (in the middle), and clay (on the top). Measure the height of each layer, as well as the overall height of the three layers. Record your measurements in Table 1.

13 Use the following formula to calculate the percentage of each kind of particle in the sample:

$$\frac{\text{height of layer}}{\text{total height of all layers}} \times 100$$

Record your results and all calculations in Table 1.

Observe and Analyze

1. **Record** Complete Table 1.

2. **Identify** How did steps 1–3 test your soil sample's pore space?

____

____

3. **Identify** How did steps 5–9 test your soil sample's drainage rate?

____

____

Conclude

1. **Evaluate** In step 3 you, measured the amount of space between the soil particles in your sample. In step 8, you measured how quickly water passed through your sample. Are these two properties related? Explain your answer.

   ____

   ____

   ____

2. **Evaluate** Would packing down or loosening up your soil sample change any of the properties you tested? Explain your answer.

   ____

   ____

   ____

3. **Interpret** What happened to the pH of the water that passed through the soil? Why do you think that happened?

   ____

   ____

   ____

4. **Analyze** Look at the percentages of sand, silt, and clay in your sample. How do the percentages help to explain the properties you observed and measured?

   ____

   ____

   ____

   ____

 ADDITIONAL INVESTIGATION
Soil Formation

OVERVIEW AND PURPOSE

As you have read, soil is a mixture of weathered rock, air, water, and organic matter. Soil forms when rocks are changed by physical, chemical, and organic processes. In this investigation you will use what you have learned about soil to

- model some of the processes that form soil
- use your "soil" to make a soil profile

Procedure

1. Put on your safety goggles. Keep them on until you have completed this entire investigation.

2. Put 4 or 5 limestone chips into the small baby food jar. Add enough vinegar to cover the chips. Screw the lid on tightly and shake the jar for 2 minutes. Let the jar stand for at least 5 minutes.

3. Put the filter paper over the beaker. Pour the contents of the jar onto the filter paper. When the liquid has been completely filtered, remove the filter paper. Put it on a sunny windowsill to dry.

4. Break off some pieces from the sandstone. Put these pieces and any sand grains onto a sheet of newspaper.

5. Put 4 or 5 limestone chips and the rest of the sandstone into the pillowcase. CAUTION: Make sure everyone is well out of your way. Use the hammer to gently crush the rocks.

6. Empty the pillowcase onto another sheet of newspaper.

MATERIALS

- 10–15 limestone chips
- small baby food jar with lid
- 250 mL white vinegar
- filter paper
- 10-mL beaker
- crumbly sandstone
- fine-grained sand
- newspaper
- old pillowcase
- hammer
- plastic tube
- laboratory spatula
- clay-rich soil
- topsoil
- small sticks and twigs
- graduated cylinder
- water
- cork to seal plastic tube
- colored pencils
- metric ruler

TIME
45 minutes

7 Most soils have at least three distinct layers. A soil profile is a cutaway view of these different layers. One kind of soil profile is shown below. You will use this drawing and the materials from this investigation to make a soil profile.

Typical Soil Profile

8 Get the plastic tube. Put a few *unaltered* limestone chips into the bottom of the tube.

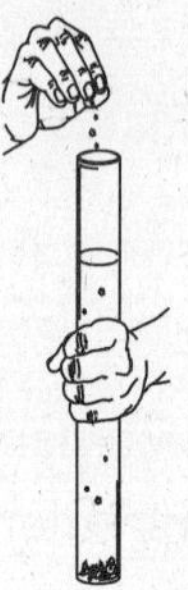

9 Add some large limestone pieces from the filter paper to the tube. Also put a few pieces of the crushed sandstone into the tube. Use the soil profile to determine how thick to make this layer.

10 Use the spatula to scrape off the powder from the filter paper. Put the powder into the tube. Put some of the sand grains in this layer as well. Add some clay. Again, use the soil profile to determine how thick to make this layer.

11 Add some topsoil and more sand grains to the tube. Break the twigs and sticks into small pieces so that they fit into the tube. Add them to your soil profile. Note that this layer is the thinnest layer in a soil profile.

12 Slowly add 5 mL of water to the tube.

13 Use the cork to seal the tube and stand it upright. Use your soil profile and the one above to answer the following questions.

Observe and Analyze

1. **Model** Which of the processes in this investigation are like the physical processes that form soil?

____

____

____

2. **Model** Which process in this investigation is similar to chemical processes that form soil?

____

____

____

____

3. **Analyze** Why does the first (bottom) layer in your profile contain unaltered rocks?

____

____

4. **Record** Use colored pencils and a metric ruler to draw your soil profile. Label and describe each layer.

CHAPTER 4 Weathering and Soil Formation

Conclude

1. **Explain** What kinds of organic matter are present in your soil?

____

____

2. **Identify Limits** How is your soil like actual soil? How is it different?

____

____

____

____

3. **Compare and Contrast** Do you think all soil profiles are the same? Why or why not?

____

____

____

____

SECTION | DATASHEET
5.1 | Investigate Erosion

How does the effect of rainwater on sloping land differ from its effect on flat land?

MATERIALS Soil, 2 large trays, pitcher of water

PROCEDURE

❶ Figure out how to use the soil, water, and trays to test the effects of rainwater on sloping land and on flat land.

❷ Write up your procedure on a separate sheet of paper.

❸ Carry out your experiment.

WHAT DO YOU THINK?

1. What were the results of your experiment? Did it work? Why or why not?

____

____

2. What were the variables in your experiment?

____

____

3. What does your experiment demonstrate about erosion and running water?

____

____

CHALLENGE

How would you design an experiment to demonstrate the relationship between floods and erosion?

____

____

____

SECTION | DATASHEET
5.3 | Investigate Longshore Drift

How does sand move along a beach?

MATERIALS 2 or 3 books, coin

PROCEDURE

❶ Prop up a book by placing another book underneath it.

❷ Hold a coin with your finger against the bottom right corner of the book.

❸ Gently flick the coin up the slope of the book at an angle. The coin should slide back down the book and fall off the bottom. If necessary, readjust the angle of the book and the strength with which you are flicking the coin.

❹ Repeat step 3 several times. Observe the path the coin takes. Record your observations. Include a diagram that shows the general path the coin takes as it slides up and down the book.

____

____

WHAT DO YOU THINK?

1. What path did the coin take on its way up? On its way down?

____

2. In this model of longshore drift, what represents the beach, what represents the sand, and what represents a wave?

____

CHALLENGE

In this model, in which direction will the longshore current move? How could you change the model to change the direction of the current?

____

____

SECTION | DATASHEET
5.4 | # Investigate Kettle Lake Formation

How do kettle lakes form?

MATERIALS shallow tray, ice cubes, modeling clay, sand, gravel, water

PROCEDURE

❶ Use the tray, the ice cubes, and the other materials to model how sediment builds up around ice blocks.

❷ Write a description of the process you used to make your model.

____

____

____

____

WHAT DO YOU THINK?

1. Describe how your model worked. What did you do first? What happened next?

____

____

____

2. Did your model accurately represent the formation of kettle lakes? Did it work? Why or why not?

____

____

____

3. What were the limitations of your model? Are there any aspects of kettle lake formation that are not represented? If so, what are they?

____

____

____

CHAPTER 5 | CHAPTER INVESTIGATION

Creating Stream Features

OVERVIEW AND PURPOSE

A view from the sky reveals that a large river twists and
bends in its channel. But as quiet as it might appear, the river
constantly digs and dumps Earth materials along its way.
This erosion and deposition causes twists and curves called
meanders, and a delta at the river's mouth. In this investigation
you will

- create a "river" in a stream table to observe the creation
  of meanders and deltas
- identify the processes of erosion and deposition

Problem

How does moving water create meanders and deltas?

Procedure

❶ Arrange the stream table on a counter so that it drains into a sink or bucket. If
possible, place a sieve beneath the outlet hose to keep sand out of the drain. You
can attach the inlet hose to a faucet if you have a proper adapter. Or you can
gently pour water in with a pitcher or use a recirculating pump and a bucket.

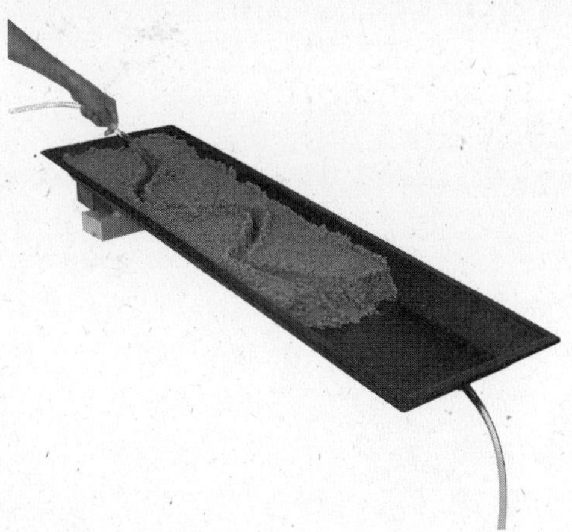

❷ Place wood blocks beneath the inlet end of the stream table so that the table tilts
toward the outlet at about a 20-degree angle. Fill the upper two-thirds of the
stream table nearly to the top with sand. Pack the sand a bit, and level the surface
with the edge of a ruler. The empty bottom third of the stream table represents the
lake or bay into which the river flows.

❸ Using the end of the ruler, dig a gently curving trench halfway through the
thickness of the sand from its upper to its lower end.

MATERIALS

- stream table, with
  hose attachment or
  recirculating pump
- sieve (optional)
- wood blocks
- sand
- ruler
- water
- sink with drain
- pitcher (optional)
- bucket (optional)

④ Direct a gentle flow of tap water into the upper end of the trench. Increase the flow slightly when the water begins to move through the trench. You may have to try this several times before you find the proper rate of flow to soak the sand and fill the stream channel. Avoid adding so much water that it pools at the top before moving into the channel. You can also change the stream table's tilt.

⑤ Once you are successful in creating a river, observe its shape and any movement of the sand. Continue until the top part of the sand is completely washed away and your river falls apart. Scrape the sand back into place with the ruler, and repeat the procedure until you thoroughly understand the stream and sand movements.

Observe and Analyze

1. **Record** Diagram your stream-table setup, and make a series of drawings showing changes in your river over time. Be sure to label the river's features, as well as areas of erosion and deposition. Be sure to diagram the behavior of the sand at the river's mouth.

2. **Record** Write a record of the development of your river from start to finish. Include details such as the degree of tilt you used, your method of introducing water into the stream table, and features you observed forming.

____

____

____

____

____

Conclude

1. **Evaluate** How do you explain the buildup of sand at the mouth of your river? Use the words *speed, erosion,* and *deposition* in your answer. Did the slope of the stream change over time?

____

____

____

____

2. **Interpret** Where in your stream table did you observe erosion occurring? Deposition? What features did each process form?

____

____

____

____

3. **Infer** What might have occurred if you had increased the amount or speed of the water flowing into your river?

____

____

____

4. **Identify Limits** In what ways was your setup a simplified version of what would actually occur on Earth? Describe the ways in which an actual stream would be more complex.

____

____

____

____

5. **Apply** Drawing on what you observed in this investigation, make two statements that relate the age of a stream to (1) the extent of its meanders and (2) to the size of its delta or alluvial fan.

____

____

____

CHAPTER | ADDITIONAL INVESTIGATION

5 | Rivers Change the Land

OVERVIEW AND PURPOSE

The moving water in a river changes Earth's landscape in different ways. A river can pick up sediments and carry them along its channel. When a river slows down, it may drop some of the sediments. In this lab, you will use what you have learned about moving water to

- observe how a river erodes and deposits sediments
- observe how the speed of a river affects the movement of sediments

Problem

How does a river change its channel?

Hypothesize

Form a hypothesis to explain how you think the speed of a river might affect the movement of sediments. Write your hypothesis as an "If . . . , then . . . , because . . . " statement.

____

____

____

MATERIALS

- long, shallow cardboard box (at least 1 m × 50 cm × 5 cm)
- large, extra-strength trash bag just larger than the cardboard box
- duct tape
- metric ruler
- marking pen
- scissors
- rubber tubing (about 1 m long)
- brick or wooden block
- bucket
- fine-grained sand (about 5 kg)
- 5–10 pieces of pea-sized gravel
- 800-mL beaker
- water

TIME: 45 minutes

Procedure

❶ Line the box with the trash bag. Push the bag completely against the bottom and sides of the box. Smooth out any wrinkles in the bag.

❷ Use pieces of duct tape to hold the bag in place.

❸ Use the ruler to mark a spot in the center of one of the short sides of the box. The spot should be about 1.5 cm from the bottom of the box.

❹ From the inside of the box, use the scissors to carefully punch a hole at the mark. The hole should be just large enough for the rubber tubing.

❺ Thread the tubing into the hole. Pull on the tubing until only about 2.5 cm of it is in the box.

6 Use the brick or block to prop up the model.

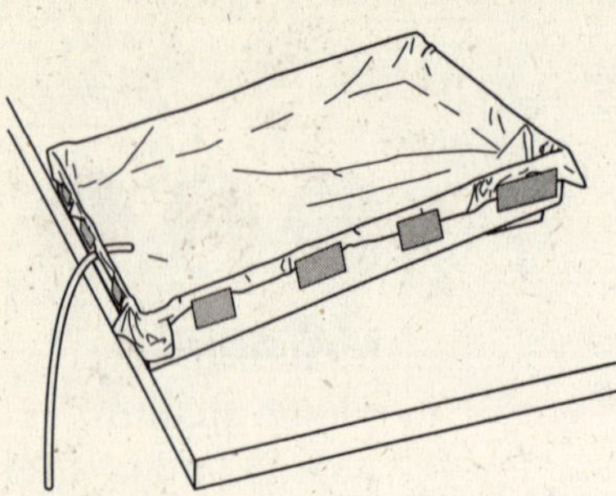

7 Put the bucket at the end of the tubing to catch the water that will flow down the model river.

8 Put the sand into the top 2/3 of the box. Level the sand, keeping it away from the tubing.

9 Use your first two fingers to carve a small channel into the sand.

10 Add a few pieces of gravel at different points in the channel.

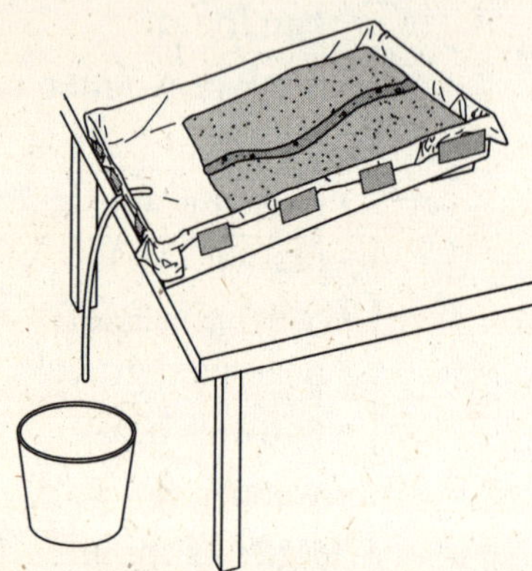

11 Fill the beaker with water. Hold it about 2.5 cm above your setup. Slowly pour the water into the channel at the top of the box.

12 Observe what happens to the sand and the gravel. Record your observations in the data table.

13 Allow the water to drain from the channel.

14 Repeat steps 11–13 three more times. Slightly increase the rate at which you pour the water into the channel each time.

DATA TABLE: RIVER FLOW OBSERVATIONS	
Trial	**Observations**
1	
2	
3	
4	

Observe and Analyze

1. Identify Variables What was your independent variable in this investigation?

____

____

____

2. Identify Variables What was your dependent variable in this investigation?

____

____

____

3. Observe During which trial was erosion the greatest?

____

____

____

4. Observe What happened to the sand transported by the model river when the moving water reached the bottom of the channel?

____

____

____

5. Analyze Was any of the gravel transported to the bottom of the channel? Why or why not?

____

____

____

Conclude

1. Compare How did your hypothesis compare with your results?

____

____

____

2. Interpret Use your results to describe three ways in which moving water can change a river channel.

____

____

____

3. Apply Where along a real river channel do you think most erosion takes place?

____

____

____

4. Conclude How does the speed of a river affect the movement of sediments?

____

____

____

5. Apply How could you change your model to increase the amount of sediment carried by the river?

____

____

____